SPOTTER'S GUIDE TO
URBAN WILDLIFE

Diana Shipp

Special Consultan
Richard Findon

Edited by Gill H

Series editors: Philippa Wingate and Sue Jacquemier
Designed by Sarah Sherley-Price
Cover design and series designer: Laura Fearn
Illustrations by Denise Finney, Dee Morgan, Andy Martin, Julie Piper
and Ian Jackson.

Consultants and contributors: Richard Scott (Landlife), Dr June
Chatfield, Dr Richard Lane, Pearl Small, Peter Smith, Alan Stubbs,
Dr Matthew M. Vriends

Picture acknowledgements: cover: from Baby Animals, pages 8-9;
backgrounds – pages 1, 2-3 © CORBIS; pages 4-23, 26-31, 34-43,
46-64 © Digital Vision.

First published in 2000 by Usborne Publishing Ltd.,
Usborne House, 83-85 Saffron Hill, London
EC1N 8RT, England. www.usborne.com

Printed in Spain

CONTENTS

4 How to use this book
6 Measuring
7 Spotting urban wildlife
8 Wild flowers
18 Trees
26 Birds
36 Mammals
39 Amphibians
40 Moths
42 Butterflies
44 Insects
49 Arachnids

50 Other invertebrates
52 Ferns and horsetail
53 Mosses
54 Fungi
56 Lichens
57 Useful words
59 Clubs and Web sites
60 Scorecard
63 Index

HOW TO USE THIS BOOK

This book is a guide to identifying some of the plants and animals that live in towns and cities in Britain and other countries of Europe. It covers trees, flowers, birds, mammals and amphibians, insects, arachnids (creatures such as spiders) and other invertebrates (animals without backbones), mosses, ferns, fungi and lichens.

The description beside each illustration tells you where the species grows or lives, or other things to help you identify it. Whenever you spot something new, put a tick in the small circle beside its description.

SCIENTIFIC NAMES
Some plants and animals have no common English name – only a scientific Latin name. The first word of the scientific name is the group to which the plant or animal belongs. The second word is the name of the species.

USEFUL WORDS
On pages 57-58, there is a list of words that you may not have come across before. Look here if you read something you don't understand.

SCORECARD
On pages 60-62, there is a scorecard that gives you a score for each plant or animal you see.

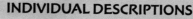

INDIVIDUAL DESCRIPTIONS

The last line of the wild flower descriptions tells you the months you usually see each plant in flower. The rest of the plant can often be seen at other times of the year.

Some trees, called deciduous trees, lose their leaves in winter. A picture in a circle next to these trees shows how they look when this happens.

With some birds and insects, the male ♂ and female ♀ look different. In this case, both sexes are illustrated and identified by their symbols.

The insects and other invertebrates are shown much bigger than they really are. Look at the measurement to check their real size.

There are many kinds of fungi, some of which are deadly poisonous. Never taste or eat any fungus unless an expert has helped you identify it.

The mosses in this book have been illustrated with the capsules that contain their spores.

5

MEASURING

The drawings on this page show you how plants and animals are measured. The measurements are average sizes, given in centimetres (cm), metres (m) or millimetres (mm). The plants and animals in this book are not drawn to scale, so this information will help you to identify the different species.

Fungi. Width of cap given in mm or cm.

Snail. Width of shell given in mm.

Butterflies, moths and bats. Wingspan given in mm or cm.

Other insects. Body length, excluding antennae, given in mm.

Spiders. Body length, not including legs, given in mm.

Other invertebrates. Body length given in mm or cm.

Birds. Length from beak to tip of tail given in cm.

Mammals and amphibians. Length of head and body, not including tail, given in cm.

Flowers, ferns, trees and mosses. Height from ground level to the top of the plant given in cm or mm.

SPOTTING URBAN WILDLIFE

At first sight it may seem that towns and cities are full of concrete, buildings and traffic and not very much else. But if you look around carefully, you will find plenty of places where wild plants and animals can and do live. More and more are adapting to urban life, so you may see things that surprise you.

Look for plants growing on walls.

Lots of different plants and creatures live on the street.

Go spotting in parks, churchyards, derelict or waste places, and along canals and rivers. Rubbish tips, playing fields, railway sidings and factory yards are also good places. Be careful not to trespass on private land and be aware of danger: don't go near derelict buildings, for example, unless you are sure they are safe.

Look closely on tree trunks and tombstones, in untidy corners of parks and gardens, in cracks in pavements and along walls. Look in and around buildings, too – many animals hide in kitchens, bathrooms, cellars and sheds during the day.

WILD FLOWERS

➡ DANDELION
This common plant grows on paths and waste places. The flowers close at night. Look for its rosette of leaves and the "clock" of downy white fruits. 5-20cm tall. March-Nov.

Dandelion "clock"

Flowers close at night

Fruiting head

Large heart-shaped leaf

◀ COLTSFOOT
Coltsfoot flowers appear before the leaves, then form a "clock" like the Dandelion. Look for woolly scales on the stalks. Grows on bare ground and waste places. 5-30cm tall. Feb-April.

Tiny leaflets between larger ones

➡ SILVERWEED
A low plant with creeping stems. New plants are formed where the stem roots. Paths, roadsides and waste places. 10-20cm tall. June-Aug.

Silvery underside to leaf

Close-up of single flower-head

◀ CANADIAN FLEABANE

This quickly spreading plant has whitish-yellow flowers. Its narrow leaves are sometimes toothed. Waste places and roadsides in southern England. Up to 1m tall. June-Oct.

➡ GROUNDSEL

Very common in waste places and on disturbed ground. Loose bunches of small yellow flowers are present all year, forming cottony seeds. Up to 45cm tall.

Leaves have wavy edges

Flowerhead

◀ PINEAPPLE WEED

A short plant that smells of pineapples. The greenish-yellow flowerheads are cone-shaped, and the leaves are feathery. Very common on paths and waste places. Up to 30cm tall. June-Sept.

WILD FLOWERS

Flowers may be pink

◀ YARROW
This plant has a rough stem and feathery leaves. The flowers form flat-topped clusters. It smells sweet, and was once used to heal wounds. Up to 40cm tall. June-Oct.

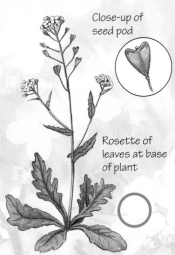

Close-up of seed pod

Rosette of leaves at base of plant

➡ SHEPHERD'S PURSE
This grows on roadsides and waste places. The white flowers and heart-shaped seed pods can be seen all year round. Up to 40cm tall.

Whorl of flowers around stem

"Hoods" on flowers

Ridges on stem

◀ WHITE DEAD-NETTLE
This looks like a Stinging Nettle, but its hairs do not sting. Its flowers grow in whorls, and it has toothed leaves. Waste places. Up to 60cm tall. May-Sept.

Sometimes flowers have no petals

◀ CHICKWEED
This plant grows anywhere where there is soil. It often forms a mat, but its stems can grow up to 40cm tall. The small flowers are present all year round.

➡ BLACK NIGHTSHADE
This is a shrubby plant with pointed oval leaves. Its petals fold back to show yellow anthers. The berries are poisonous. Up to 50cm tall. July-Oct.

Poisonous berries

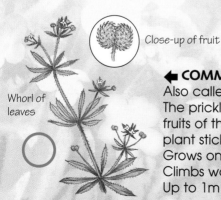

Close-up of fruit

Whorl of leaves

◀ COMMON CLEAVERS
Also called Goosegrass. The prickly stems and fruits of this scrambling plant stick to clothes. Grows on waste ground. Climbs walls and fences. Up to 1m tall. May-Aug.

WILD FLOWERS

➡ RIBWORT PLANTAIN
This is a tough, common plant with narrow, ribbed leaves. It has short green-brown spikes of flowers with whitish anthers. 20cm tall. April-Sept.

Flowers

Anthers

Deeply-furrowed stem

Ribs on leaves

Anthers are mauve at first, changing to yellow

No furrows on stem

Ribs on leaves

⬅ GREATER PLANTAIN
This has a long, greenish spike of flowers and broad, ribbed leaves in a rosette near the ground. Paths and waste places. 15cm tall. May-Sept.

➡ WHITE CLOVER
This plant creeps along the ground, often on roadside verges. Look for the white band on the three-lobed leaf. Attracts bees. 10-30cm tall. May-Sept.

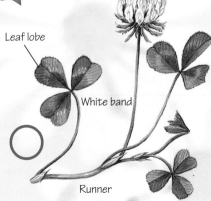

White or pinkish flowers

Leaf lobe

White band

Runner

White petals are sometimes tinged with pink

← DAISY

Small plant with a rosette of leaves at base. Its flowers close at night and in bad weather. Found in most grassy places. 10cm tall. Feb-Nov.

→ HEDGE BINDWEED

Climbs walls and fences in waste places. Its stems twist anti-clockwise and its large, bell-shaped flowers close at night. 3m high. June-Sept.

Twisting stem

Bud

Flowers are sometimes pink

Close-up of flower

Tiny flowers

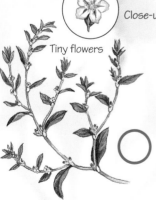

← KNOTGRASS

A weed that may spread in a thick mat or grow erect. Flowers may be pink, white or green. Stems can be 1m long. Waste places and bare ground. June-Oct.

13

WILD FLOWERS

➡ **COMMON MALLOW**
Can be erect or
sprawling. It grows in
derelict and waste
places, and often attracts
bees. Stems up to 90cm
long. June-Sept.

Notch in petal

Seed with hairy
"parachute"

Buds

⬅ **ROSEBAY
WILLOWHERB**
This tall, erect plant is also
called Fireweed. It has
spikes of pink flowers and
long, narrow leaves.
Common on waste
ground. Up to 1m tall.
July-Sept.

Hairy seeds
are inside
long pods

Leaves are
hairy

➡ **GREAT WILLOWHERB**
Also known as Codlins-
and-Cream. Grows near
canals, ponds and in
damp places. About 1m
tall with a hairy stem and
hairy seeds. July-Aug.

14

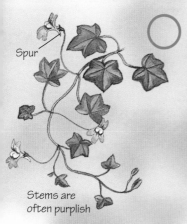

Spur

Stems are often purplish

➤ BLACKBERRY

This dense, woody plant climbs up fences and walls or trails along the ground. Has sharp prickles on stems and leaves. May-Nov.

◄ IVY-LEAVED TOADFLAX

The weak, slender stalks of this plant trail on old walls. Look for the yellow patches on the mauve flowers, which are 10mm across. Small shiny leaves. May-Sept.

Flower bud

Ripe berry

Stem has large thorns

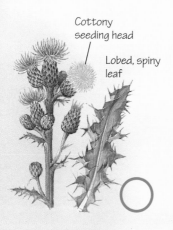

Cottony seeding head

Lobed, spiny leaf

◄ CREEPING THISTLE

A creeping plant with stems that may be over 1m long. Its fragrant mauve flowers attract insects. Derelict and waste places. July-Sept.

15

WILD FLOWERS

➤ STINGING NETTLE
The toothed leaves are covered with stinging hairs, and it has dangling spikes of green-brown flowers. Grows up to 1m tall. June-Sept.

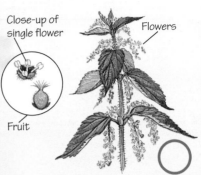

Close-up of single flower

Flowers

Fruit

Main, lower leaves are thick and diamond-shaped

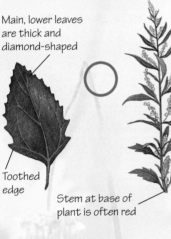

Toothed edge

Stem at base of plant is often red

◄ FAT HEN
A dark green, stiff plant. Its stems often look reddish. The young shoots have a whitish covering. Common in waste places. Up to 1m tall. July-Oct.

Flowers may be yellowish or purplish-brown

➤ MUGWORT
A tall, slightly fragrant plant. The leaves look silky and silvery underneath. Common in waste places and by roads. About 1m high. July-Sept.

Greyish leaves

16

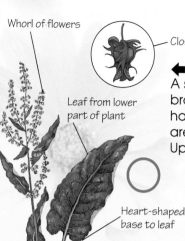

Whorl of flowers

Close-up of fruit

Leaf from lower part of plant

◀ BROAD-LEAVED DOCK
A sturdy plant with large broad leaves that are often hairy underneath. Its fruits are toothed. Waste places. Up to 1m high. June-Oct.

Heart-shaped base to leaf

Close-up of flower

➡ CURLED DOCK
The long, narrow leaves of this plant have very wavy edges, hence its name. It has untoothed oval fruits. Up to 1m high. June-Oct.

Fruit

Whorl of flowers

Leaf from lower part of plant

◀ IVY
An evergreen woody plant that climbs up trees, fences and walls. Its glossy leaves often have pale veins. Has black berries in winter. Sept-Nov.

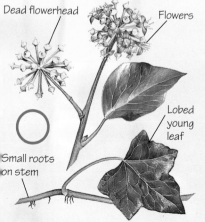

Dead flowerhead

Flowers

Lobed young leaf

Small roots on stem

17

TREES

Needles are parted on twig

↑ YEW

You often see this plant in churchyards. It has red berry-like fruits and orange-brown flaking bark. New light green needles turn dark green with age. Up to 25m tall.

Poisonous berry

Long blunt bud

Short paired needles

Green cone ripens to brown in second year

↑ SCOTS PINE

This tree has short blue-green paired needles. Its upper bark is orangey, but grey and furrowed lower down. 35m tall.

Sparse-looking crown

↑ LONDON PLANE

Plane trees are often planted in streets. They have large broad leaves with pointed lobes and spiny "bobble" fruits. The bark flakes, leaving yellowish patches. 30m tall.

Ripe fruit

Large lobed leaf has toothed edge

Fruits twist as they fall

↑ SYCAMORE

Look for dark green, leathery leaves with five lobes, and paired, closely-angled winged seeds. The bark becomes scaly. 25-30m tall.

19

TREES

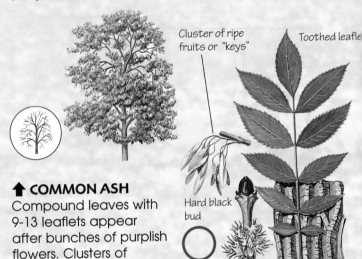

Cluster of ripe fruits or "keys"

Toothed leaflet

↑ COMMON ASH
Compound leaves with 9-13 leaflets appear after bunches of purplish flowers. Clusters of "keys" last into the winter. 30-40m tall.

Hard black bud

Flowers

Broad crown

Toothed edge

Leafy wing

Young fruits

Round leaf with small point

↑ COMMON LIME
A common tree in roads, parks and churchyards. Its yellowish-green, sweet-smelling flowers attract large numbers of insects in July. 25-35m tall.

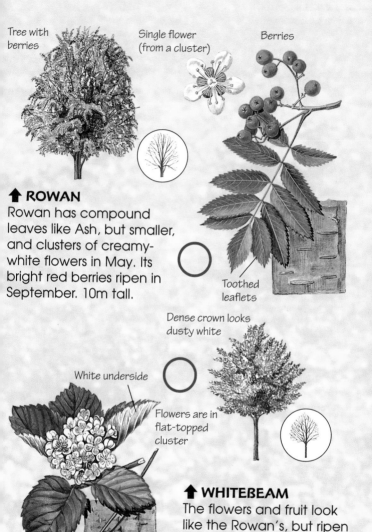

Tree with berries

Single flower (from a cluster)

Berries

↑ ROWAN

Rowan has compound leaves like Ash, but smaller, and clusters of creamy-white flowers in May. Its bright red berries ripen in September. 10m tall.

Toothed leaflets

Dense crown looks dusty white

White underside

Flowers are in flat-topped cluster

↑ WHITEBEAM

The flowers and fruit look like the Rowan's, but ripen later. The oval leaves have toothed edges and are white and furry underneath. 10-15m tall.

Berries

21

TREES

Tree in bloom

Leaves have 5-7 leaflets

Flowers

↑ HORSE CHESTNUT

Has a compound leaf of 5-7 large leaflets, and an upright "candle" of white (or pink) flowers in May. Parks and avenues. 25m tall.

Conker (fruit) is in prickly case

Smooth-edged leaflet

↑ FALSE ACACIA

Has compound leaves of many small leaflets, pairs of sharp thorns on twigs and deeply-furrowed bark. White flowers hang in clusters in June. 20m tall.

Strong-smelling flowers

Tree is in bloom
June-July

Soft bark

Cluster of ripe
berries (Aug-Sept)

↑ ELDER
Several stems arch up
from ground. Has
compound leaves of 3-9
toothed leaflets. Its flat
clusters of whitish flowers
develop into black
berries. 7m tall.

Tapering pointed tip

Black diamond
shapes on trunk

↑ SILVER BIRCH
A slender tree with
drooping branches. Has
small leaves with double-
toothed edge, and long
"lamb's tail" catkins in
April. 15m tall.

Silvery
peeling bark

23

TREES

Young seed pods are green

Tree is in bloom May-June

Soft, hairy leaflets

↑ LABURNAM

This small tree grows in streets, parks and gardens. Its leaf is made up of three leaflets. It has hanging clusters of yellow flowers and poisonous seeds in twisted pods. 7m tall.

Bronze-coloured young leaf

Tree is in bloom April-May

Sharply-toothed edge

↑ JAPANESE CHERRY ('KANZAN')

Seen in parks and streets. Its leaves are pointed and its bark has a metallic sheen. Pink blossom in spring. 9m tall.

Only some trees
have berries

Two kinds of flower

⬆ HOLLY

Has shiny, dark, leathery
evergreen leaves with
thorny prickles. Small
white flowers in summer
are followed by red
berries. It can be a small
tree or a shrub. 10m tall.

Branches grow
upwards

Leaf shape varies

⬆ LOMBARDY
POPLAR

Tall narrow tree
often planted along
roadsides. The branches
grow upwards from near
the ground. Has pointed
triangular leaves. 28m tall.

Furrowed bark

25

BIRDS

➡ PIED/WHITE WAGTAIL

The White Wagtail is widespread in Europe, but in Britain we usually see only the Pied Wagtail. However, they are very difficult to tell apart. Common in towns and near water. 18cm.

Summer plumage

Winter plumage

White undertail

⬅ MOORHEN

A water bird that lives near ponds, lakes or canals. Easy to recognise because of its red bill and white tail. Eats seeds, insects, and tadpoles. 33cm.

Line of white streaks

Green legs

White bill and "forehead"

➡ COOT

Found on lakes in town parks. Dives under water to feed on plants. Has large feet, but not webbed like a duck's. 38cm.

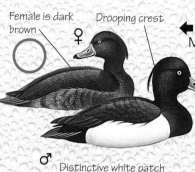

Female is dark brown ♀

Drooping crest

◀ TUFTED DUCK
More common in winter. Often forms large groups. Feeds underwater on plants and animals. Can be seen on ponds in parks. 43cm.

♂ Distinctive white patch

▶ MALLARD
Very common on town ponds, lakes and canals. Often upends, but also feeds on water surface. Only the female "quacks" loudly. 58cm.

♂ ♀

Here, wings are arched in threat; usually flat against back

◀ MUTE SWAN
Often seen in town parks or on canals. Not mute (which means silent), as its name suggests. Orange bill has knob at base. 150cm.

BIRDS

➡ BLACK-HEADED GULL
This bird has a dark brown head in summer, and a pale head with a dark spot behind the eye in winter. Common inland and near the sea. 37cm.

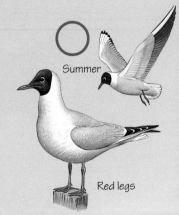

Summer

Red legs

Summer

Red spot on bill

⬅ HERRING GULL
Common on the coast; seen inland mostly in winter, feeding on refuse. It nests on buildings. The young are mottled brown at first, becoming greyer. 56cm.

Black wing tips

Pink legs

➡ KESTREL
Well known for the way it hovers when hunting, especially alongside roads. In towns, it often eats small birds. May nest in buildings or trees. 34cm.

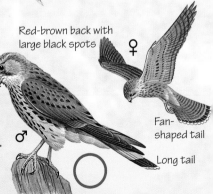

Red-brown back with large black spots

♀

Fan-shaped tail

Long tail

♂

White on wings

Small round head

← WOODPIGEON
In towns, this bird becomes very tame and often mixes with Feral Pigeons. Look for the white patches on its neck and wings. Forms large flocks. 41cm.

→ FERAL PIGEON
These common birds are domestic pigeons that have gone wild. They are descended from the wild Rock Dove, which nests on cliffs. Feral Pigeons nest on man-made cliffs – the ledges of buildings. Plumage can vary a lot. 33cm.

Often has white patches on wings

Plumage can be blue, grey, brown, white or chequered

Black half-collar on neck

Long, white tail with black base

← COLLARED DOVE
Found in parks or large gardens, and nests in trees and on ledges. it eats seeds, berries and scraps. Sometimes seen in flocks. 30cm.

29

BIRDS

➡ SWIFT
A common summer visitor (migrant) that visits Britain in May-Aug. Flies fast over towns catching insects. Listen for its screaming call. 17cm.

Forked tail is often closed to form a single point

Long curved wings

White underparts

⬅ SWALLOW
This summer migrant is seen from April-Oct. It often feeds on insects over water. It builds its nest on rafters or ledges in buildings. 19cm.

Glossy blue back often looks black

➡ HOUSE MARTIN
Also a summer migrant. It builds a cup-shaped nest under eaves of houses and under bridges, and often lives in small colonies. Catches insects in flight. Look for its white rump. 13cm.

Broad white patch on rump

Has brilliant white underparts

Brownish wings

Young Starling

Adult in winter

Short, square tail

◀ STARLING
Common even in the centre of large cities. In winter, the resident population in Britain is joined by millions of migrants from north and east Europe. 22cm.

➡ ROBIN
The Robin sings its sweet-sounding song during winter and spring. Its alarm call is "tic-tic". Male and female Robins look alike. 14cm.

Red breast and face

◀ SONG THRUSH
This bird eats snails, breaking open the shells on a rock known as its "anvil". It also eats worms, insects and berries. Found near, or in, trees or bushes. 23cm.

BIRDS

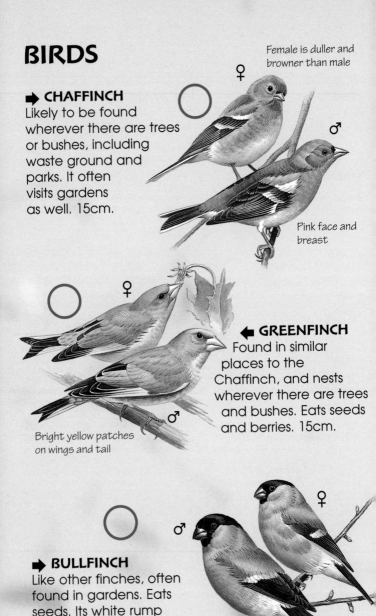

Female is duller and browner than male

♀

➤ CHAFFINCH
Likely to be found wherever there are trees or bushes, including waste ground and parks. It often visits gardens as well. 15cm.

♂

Pink face and breast

♀

◄ GREENFINCH
Found in similar places to the Chaffinch, and nests wherever there are trees and bushes. Eats seeds and berries. 15cm.

♂

Bright yellow patches on wings and tail

♂   ♀

➤ BULLFINCH
Like other finches, often found in gardens. Eats seeds. Its white rump shows in flight. 15cm.

← HOUSE SPARROW
Lives near houses and even in city centres, where it eats scraps and crumbs. The colour of birds in cities may be duller than shown here. 15cm.

→ DUNNOCK
This bird has a slate-grey face and breast. Look for it under bushes, where it creeps about looking for insects and seeds. 14.5cm.

Often flicks its wings

Often cocks its tail up

Very small bird

← WREN
Found in all kinds of places including parks and gardens. Loud song finishes with a trill. Never stays still for long. 9.5cm.

BIRDS

➡ BLUE TIT
Seen in parks, gardens and churchyards. Often raises its blue cap to form a small crest. The young are less colourful than the adults. 11cm.

Blue cap

Narrow dark stripe

Blue wings with white bar

Black head

Broad dark stripe

⬅ GREAT TIT
This bird is not quite as common as the Blue Tit, but it is seen in similar places. it nests in holes in trees and will nest in nesting boxes. 14cm.

➡ BLACKBIRD
Lives where there are trees and bushes, often in parks, gardens and waste places. Has a loud alarm call. 25cm.

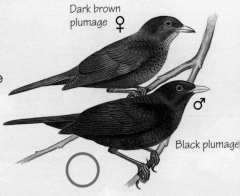

Dark brown plumage ♀

Black plumage ♂

34

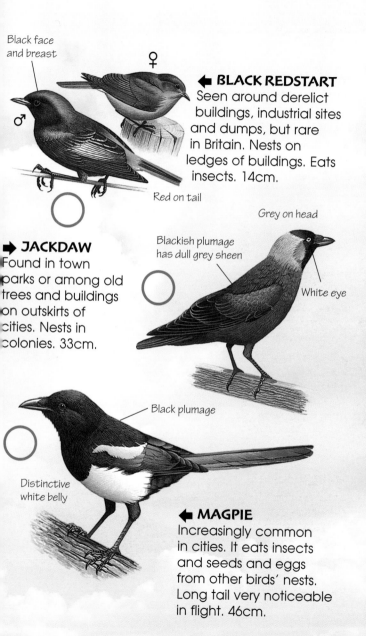

Black face and breast

♀

♂

◀ BLACK REDSTART
Seen around derelict buildings, industrial sites and dumps, but rare in Britain. Nests on ledges of buildings. Eats insects. 14cm.

Red on tail

Grey on head

➡ JACKDAW
Found in town parks or among old trees and buildings on outskirts of cities. Nests in colonies. 33cm.

Blackish plumage has dull grey sheen

White eye

Black plumage

Distinctive white belly

◀ MAGPIE
Increasingly common in cities. It eats insects and seeds and eggs from other birds' nests. Long tail very noticeable in flight. 46cm.

MAMMALS

Short tail

MOLE
Lives underground, but occasionally comes to the surface. Molehills are piles of earth from its tunnels. Not found in Ireland. Body length 13cm.

Strong claws for digging

HEDGEHOG
Hedgehogs are mainly nocturnal, and hibernate in winter. When alarmed, they roll into a ball. They eat animals such as worms and slugs, and they often snuffle, squeal and snore. Body length 25cm.

Sharp prickles on back

Hair underneath

Small bat with jerky flight

PIPISTRELLE BAT
Often seen in town parks and squares after sunset, when it catches insects on the wing. Rests during the day in hollow trees and buildings. Wingspan 20-30cm. Body length 5cm.

Soft fur

Roosting bat

➡ BROWN RAT

Brown rats eat more or less anything. In winter they live in buildings; in summer, they move to sewers, canals and river banks. Max. body length 26cm.

Fur is usually brown and rather shaggy

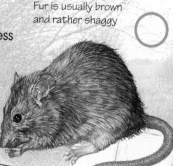

Shorter, fatter tail than black rat

Larger ears than brown rat

Sleek fur

⬅ BLACK RAT

This rat is rare, and is found only near ports and coastal towns. It lives in the tops of buildings such as warehouses. It is nocturnal and eats anything. Max. body length 20cm.

Fur may be black or brown

Slender tail

➡ HOUSE MOUSE

The indoor variety is grey, outdoor ones are browner. They eat stored food and grain, and make buildings smell musty. Mostly nocturnal. Body length 9cm.

MAMMALS

➡ COMMON SHREW
This fast-moving mammal lives in thick grass or bushes and eats insects and worms. It may nest under rubbish. Not found in Ireland. Body length 7cm.

Long, pointed muzzle

⬅ GREY SQUIRREL
Squirrels are common in parks and gardens and can become very bold and tame. Their coats may have brown patches. Body length 27cm.

➡ RABBIT
Rabbits often live in large groups on grassy wasteland, in burrows underground. They feed on plants, and are active at dusk and dawn. Body length 40cm.

← FOX
Increasingly common in towns, where they scavenge for food from dustbins and rubbish tips. Mainly nocturnal. Body length 65cm.

Bushy tail

AMPHIBIANS

➡ COMMON FROG
Common in gardens, especially wet, shady corners or ponds. They mate and lay their eggs ("spawn") in water. The tadpoles hatch from eggs and grow into adult frogs. Up to 10cm long.

Shiny skin

♂

Spawn

Tadpole

Dull, warty skin

♂

← COMMON TOAD
Like frogs, toads often live in gardens. They can swim, but only go into the water to breed. Tadpoles develop in same way as Frog tadpoles. Female up to 13cm long, male much smaller.

Tadpole

39

MOTHS

Head

← ELEPHANT HAWK MOTH
Found on waste places, even in city centres. The larva's head tapers like an elephant's trunk, and it eats Willowherb and Fuschia.
Wingspan 65mm.

♂ ♀

→ VAPOURER MOTH
Common all over Britain. Found anywhere in towns where there are a few trees. Female has only wing stubs and cannot fly. Wingspan 35mm.

Hind wings often look pink

Ragwort

← CINNABAR MOTH
Often flies by day, but weakly. Striped larvae feed in groups on Ragwort. Common on waste ground and railway banks. Wingspan 40-45mm.

➡ LARGE YELLOW UNDERWING

Sometimes flies into houses at night. Rests in Ivy on walls during day. Larva eats grasses and other small plants. Common everywhere. Wingspan 45-60mm.

⬅ GARDEN TIGER MOTH

The larva is more often seen than the adult moth. Found near vegetation in all kinds of places including paths and gardens. Wingspan 65mm.

Larva is called "woolly bear"

➡ SIX-SPOT BURNET MOTH

This moth, and the similar Five-spot Burnet, flies by day over grassy areas. Wingspan 35mm.

Larva on Vetch; it also eats Clover and Bird's-foot Trefoil

BUTTERFLIES

➡ PAINTED LADY

Arrives in spring from the Mediterranean. Adults cannot survive winter in Britain, so may fly south in autumn. Wingspan 62-65mm.

Lays eggs on thistles

◀ RED ADMIRAL

Common in waste places, on Buddleia and Michaelmas Daisies. Migrates here from the Mediterranean. Its larvae feed on nettles. Wingspan 66-68mm.

➡ SMALL TORTOISESHELL

This butterfly visits many flowers and is common all over Britain. Its name comes from the pattern on its wings. It has two broods, and its larvae feed on nettles. Wingspan 48-52mm.

Blue dots on edge of wings

➡ SMALL WHITE

Common in waste places,
parks and gardens. It
appears in April-May
and August. Lays single
eggs on cabbages and
Nasturtiums. Wingspan
48-50mm.

♂

♀

♀

♂

⬇ PEACOCK

This butterfly hibernates as
an adult in places such as
hollow trees and sheds. It
lays its eggs on nettles, and
its larvae spin webs.
Wingspan 62-68mm.

Markings look like
the "eyes" on a
peacock's tail

INSECTS

➡ COMMON WASP
Wasps live in big colonies and kill their prey by stinging. They are attracted by food, and are often seen around dustbins. 11-20mm long.

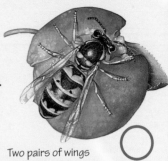

Two pairs of wings

Leaf cut by bee

⬅ LEAF-CUTTER BEE
This bee cuts semi-circular pieces from rose leaves to make cylinders, where the female lays a single egg provided with nectar and pollen. Male 10mm long, female 11mm.

➡ BUFF-TAILED BUMBLEBEE
Very few survive the winter. Usually lives in a colony underground. 11-22mm long.

One pair of wings

⬅ HOVERFLY
Looks like a small wasp, but it has only two wings and does not sting. On sunny days, it hovers then darts off quickly. Larvae eat aphids. 11-14mm long.

◄ COMMON CRANEFLY

Also called Daddy-long-legs. Sometimes flies into houses at night. Does not bite or sting. Larvae, called Leatherjackets, are found in lawns. Adult is 17-25mm long.

Very long legs

➤ HOUSEFLY

Very common. Attracted by food and rubbish, and can carry diseases. Larvae are legless maggots. 7-8mm long.

Grey and brown body

➤ BLOWFLY

This is more commonly called the Bluebottle. It makes a loud buzzing sound, and lays eggs on dead animals or on meat left uncovered. Seen March-Oct. 9-15mm long.

Blue, hairy body

Larva catching aphid

◄ GREEN LACEWING

Sometimes attracted to house lights, and often hibernates in houses and garden sheds. Its larvae eat aphids. 15mm long.

INSECTS

➡ COMMON FROGHOPPER
Good at jumping. The nymph lives on plant juices, forming a froth ("cuckoo spit") on stems. Adult is 5-6mm long.

Nymph is inside "spit"

Adult on blade of grass

⬅ GREENFLY
A kind of green or pinkish aphid. They can be a pest on roses in spring. They produce honeydew, which ants feed on. 2-3mm long.

Rose twig

➡ COMMON COCKROACH
Lives in houses and other warm buildings, where it eats waste. Females lay eggs in purse-like containers. Active at night. 25mm long.

Bread

Bread

⬅ GERMAN COCKROACH
Now more common than the Common Cockroach. Lives in places such as restaurants, hospitals and bakeries. Hides during the day. 13mm long.

➡ TWO-SPOT LADYBIRD

Very common. Colour
pattern often varies –
some individuals
are shiny black
with red spots.
4-5mm long.

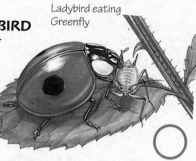

Ladybird eating
Greenfly

⬅ SEVEN-SPOT LADYBIRD

Very common in parks and
waste places. Spends the
winter in houses, sheds or
trees under bark. Comes
out on sunny spring days,
and is seen throughout
the summer. 6-7mm long.

➡ DEVIL'S COACH-HORSE

Eats larvae, slugs and
snails. It can ooze
poisonous liquid
from the end of
its abdomen. If
challenged, it
raises its tail and
spreads its jaws.
25-30mm long.

Adult

Larva

INSECTS

➡ SILVERFISH
Wingless insect that lives in old houses, especially bathrooms and kitchens. Active at night. Runs to shelter when light is turned on. About 10mm long.

Shiny, silvery body

Runs very quickly on tiny legs

➡ COMMON EARWIG
Eats small, usually dead insects, leaves and fruit. Female guards larvae until they can look after themselves. 15mm long.

♂ ♀

Forceps are raised when earwig is threatened

⬅ HOUSE CRICKET
Often found in new buildings and on rubbish tips. Makes a chirping sound. Has large hind legs for jumping. 20mm long.

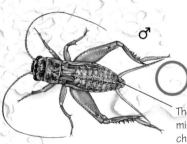

♂

The male's hind wings may be missing (as here) – the female chews them off during mating

➡ BLACK ANT
Lives under paving stones and rocks. May go into houses in search of sweet food. Winged male and female ants swarm in autumn. 3-9mm long.

Winged ants

Wingless worker ant

ARACHNIDS

➡ HARVESTMAN
Very common around buildings, especially in autumn. Hunts at night for insects and spiders. Female lays eggs in the ground. Body 4-9mm long.

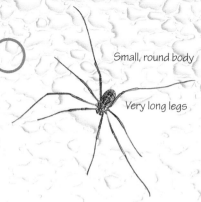

Small, round body

Very long legs

Short legs

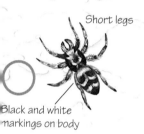

Black and white markings on body

⬅ ZEBRA SPIDER
Does not spin a web but jumps on its prey. Often seen hunting on walls on sunny days. Its markings are for camouflage, Body 4-7mm long.

➡ GARDEN SPIDER
Spins a web to catch flies and other insects. Often hangs head-down in the middle of its web. Female is much larger than the male. Body 7-18mm long.

White pattern on body

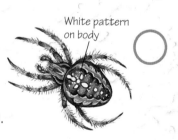

Brown, hairy body

⬅ HOUSE SPIDER
Large spider that lives in houses and sheds. Often falls into baths. Spins a tangled web in odd corners. Body 9-14mm long.

OTHER INVERTEBRATES

➡ GARDEN SLUG
Most often seen after rain on summer nights, on soil or wet paths. Spends daytime in shady damp places. Burrows to feed on roots. 25-30mm long.

Leaves yellow-orange slimy trail

Thick black line and groove on side

Breathing hole

⬅ NETTED SLUG
Very common. Leaves a white slimy trail. Eats fruit, leaves and roots of plants – a serious garden pest. 35mm long.

Mottled with darker markings

➡ GARDEN SNAIL
Hides under stones during the day, then comes out to feed on plants at night. Shell is 25-35mm across.

Large, thick shell

Greyish body

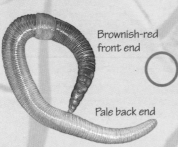

Brownish-red front end

Pale back end

⬅ EARTHWORM
Burrows in soil, eating dead plant matter. Pulls in leaves to plug up the end of its burrow. Often seen on the surface after rain. 10-30cm long.

← WOODLOUSE
Oniscus asellus
Lives in damp places,
including cellars. May be
grey or yellowish with
paler patches. Active at
night. 15-18mm long.

→ WOODLOUSE
Porcellio scaber
Usually grey, sometimes
has black dots. Lives in
cellars, under stones
and bark. Eats plants.
11-18mm long.

Legs are lighter
brown than body

← CENTIPEDE
Lives under stones or in
damp, dark places like
cellars. Sometimes seen in
baths. Can poison and
kill insects and slugs
with its front claws.
18-30mm long.

→ SNAKE
MILLIPEDE
Lives in soil, under stones
or in other dark places.
Eats plant roots. Active at
night. Sometimes
enters houses.
20-30mm long.

Cylindrical body

Has about one
hundred pairs of legs

FERNS AND HORSETAIL

➡ WALL RUE
The dull green, leathery fronds grow in tufts from the underground stem on long stalks. Grows on old limestone walls, particularly churches. 2-15cm tall.

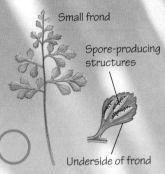

Small frond

Spore-producing structures

Underside of frond

Large frond

Kidney-shaped coverings hide spore-producing structures

◀ MALE FERN
Common and widespread on the tops of walls, drains and other shady places. Its large fronds usually die back in autumn. 40-100cm tall.

Underside of frond

Sections of branches break off easily

Fertile stem produces spores

Ridges on stem

Whorl of branches

➡ FIELD HORSETAIL
Pinkish-brown fertile stems appear in spring. Larger, green shoots with whorls of branches appear later. Waste places. 10-90cm tall.

MOSSES

➡ BEARD MOSS
A short-stemmed moss which forms small mats or cushions on tops of walls and on bare ground. The leaves are small and blunt, without hairs. 1cm tall.

➡ WALL SCREW MOSS
Forms small short cushions that look grey when dry. The hairy pointed leaves twist up when dry, and form rosettes when moist. Common on walls. Up to 1cm tall.

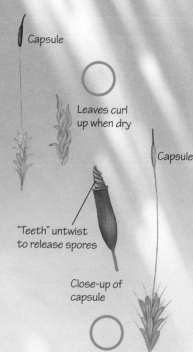

Capsule

Leaves curl up when dry

Capsule

"Teeth" untwist to release spores

Close-up of capsule

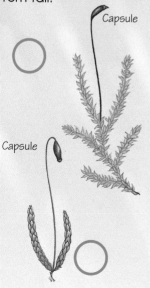

Capsule

Capsule

⬅ BRACHYTHECIUM RUTABULUM
Grows in large, straggly tufts. Glossy green or yellow branches grow out irregularly from creeping stems. Common in lawns. Up to 5cm tall.

⬅ SILVER CORD MOSS
Grows on wall-tops and between cracks in pavements, where little else grows. Dark green leaves have a silvery sheen. 5-15mm tall.

FUNGI

➡ COMMON INK CAP
Grows at the base of broad-leaved trees, in gardens and on bare ground. The gills (on underside) are whitish at first, then brown. Cap 3-7cm wide.

Ribs

Ring-like zones at base of stem

Rings of colour on cap

◀ CORIOLUS VERSICOLOR
Brightly coloured fungus with velvet-like cap, seen all year round. Grows in layers on cut stumps and branches of broad-leaved trees. Cap 2-5cm wide.

Pale edge

Small pores under cap

Section of underside of Coriolus versicolor

➡ CORAL SPOT FUNGUS
Grows on damp twigs and dead branches of trees all year round. The groups of small pale pink dots gradually turn dark red-brown. 3-4mm across.

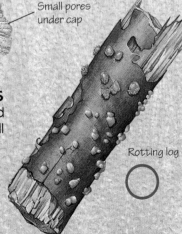

Rotting log

Cream-brown cap
can split with age

DO NOT TASTE ANY FUNGUS WITHOUT EXPERT ADVICE

White pores

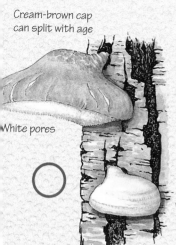

← BIRCH POLYPORE
The flesh of this fungus
was once used as
blotting paper, and to
stop bleeding. Grows all
year round on Birch
trees, which it kills.
Cap 5-30cm.

White cap when young

Orange tint at
centre of cap

➡ SULPHUR TUFT
Grows in clusters on
and around stumps
of broad-leaved
trees, often in large
numbers. It has a
faint ring on the
stem, yellow flesh
and purple-brown
pores. Cap 4-10cm.
Aug-Nov.

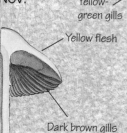

Yellow-
green gills

Yellow flesh

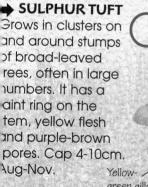

Dark brown gills
when old

Stem is darker at base

LICHENS

Fruiting structures

← COMMON ORANGE LICHEN
An easily spotted disc-like lichen that forms patches on roofs, tombstones and walls. The patches are about 15cm across.

➡ GREY CRUST LICHEN
The most common crust lichen of town centres. It forms an inconspicuous thick crust with no clear edges. Found on walls, pavements, tombstones, and trees.

Forms a thick crust with powdery surface

← PARMELIA PHYSODES
A leafy kind of lichen common on fences, walls, trees or soil. It forms bluish-grey patches of narrow lobes with swollen ends. It is dark grey or black underneath

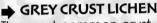

USEFUL WORDS

abdomen – the hind section of an insect.

amphibians – animals that are born in water but spend most of their adult life on land.

anther – the part of a flower that produces pollen.

aphid – a type of insect, such as Greenfly or Blackfly.

arachnid – a particular kind of invertebrate that has four pairs of legs, such as a spider.

camouflage – the colouring or pattern on an animal that allows it to blend into its background, so that it is difficult to see.

cap (of fungi) – the part of some fungi that sits on top of a stalk.

capsule (of moss) – the part of the moss that contains the spores.

catkin – a hanging cluster of tiny flowers, found on some trees.

colony – a group of plants or animals living together.

colonise – the process by which plants and animals move to live in new areas.

compound leaf – a leaf that is made up of several small leaflets.

crown (of tree) – the top branches and leaves.

deciduous - a tree that loses its leaves in winter.

evergreen – a tree that doesn't lose its leaves in winter, the opposite of a deciduous tree.

frond – the leaf-like part of a fern.

fruit – the part of a plant that contains the seed, or seeds.

gills (of fungi) – the ribs on the underside of some fungi, which radiate out from the stem like the spokes of a wheel.

hibernation – when some animals spend the winter in an inactive state with a lower body temperature than usual, allowing them to survive without eating.

honeydew – the sweet liquid produced by some insects.

invertebrates – animals without backbones – for example, insects, spiders and worms.

larva (plural: **larvae**) – the form which some insects and other animals take before they become adult, for example caterpillars of moths and butterflies.

leaflet – a small leaf that forms part of a compound leaf.

lobe – a part that sticks out from the central part of a flower or leaf.

migrant – an animal that regularly travels to another area or country.

native (to Britain) – a species of plant or animal that has not been introduced by man.

nocturnal – active mostly at night.

nymph – a kind of insect larva (*see* **larva**).

plumage – the general term for a bird's feathers.

rosette – a ring of leaves, usually growing close to the ground, around the stem of a plant.

runner (of a plant) – a stem that creeps over the surface of the ground, rooting at intervals and producing a new plant.

scavenge – to hunt for food amongst rubbish and left-overs, as foxes and rats do.

shrub – a woody plant, usually smaller than a tree, with several main branches instead of a trunk.

spawn – the eggs of an amphibian – eg a frog or toad.

spores – the tiny reproductive cells of plants such as ferns, mosses, fungi and lichens, that do not produce seeds: often produced in thousands of millions.

tadpole – the stage an amphibian lives at between hatching from spawn and becoming an adult.

whorl – a ring of three or more leaves or flowers around the stem of a plant.

CLUBS AND WEB SITES

Joining a conservation club or society is a good way to learn more about wildlife and to meet other people who share your interests. Here are some organizations you can contact.

The British Naturalists' Association
48 Russel Way,
Higham Ferrers,
Northamptonshire
NN9 8EJ

Landlife
Court Hey Park,
Liverpool L16 3NA

The Wildlife Trusts
The Kiln,
Waterside,
Mather Road,
Newark,
Nottinghamshire
NG24 1WT

BTCV (British Trust for Conservation Volunteers)
36 St Mary's St,
Wallingford,
Oxfordshire
OX10 0EU

You will be able to find lots more information about wildlife on-line. Here are some Web sites to visit.

The Postcode Plants Database – Use your postcode to search for a list of birds and animals that live in your area, as well as wild flowers.
http://fff.nhm.ac.uk/fff/

The Wildlife Trusts – Information about local Wildlife Trust groups across the UK, including Urban groups.
http://www.wildlifetrust.org.uk/

BTCV – Details of opportunities to join conservation projects as a volunteer in your area.
http://www.btcv.org.uk/

Wharfe – Links to a Wild Flower Page and many other environmental organizations.
http://www.wharfe.demon.co.uk/

SCORECARD

Everything on this scorecard is arranged in alphabetical order. Rare species score more than common ones. When you spot a species, fill in the date next to it. After a day's spotting, make a note of the points you have scored. See if you can score more points another day.

Species	Score	Date spotted	Species	Score	Date spotted
Beard moss	10		Cinnabar moth	15	
Black ant	5		Collared dove	10	
Blackberry	5		Coltsfoot	5	
Blackbird	5		Common ash	5	
Black-headed gull	5		Common cleavers	5	
Black nightshade	15		Common cockroach	10	
Black rat	25		Common cranefly	5	
Black redstart	25		Common earwig	5	
Blowfly	5		Common frog	10	
Blue tit	5		Common froghopper	10	
Brachythecium rutabulum	5		Common ink-cap	15	
Broad-leaved dock	5		Common lime	10	
Brown rat	5		Common mallow	5	
Buff-tailed bumblebee	5		Common orange lichen	15	
Bullfinch	10		Common shrew	15	
Canadian fleabane	15		Common toad	15	
Centipede	5		Common wasp	10	
Chaffinch	5		Coot	5	
Chickweed	5		Coral spot fungus	10	

Species	Score	Date spotted	Species	Score	Date spotted
Coriolus versicolor	10		Grey crust lichen	5	
Creeping thistle	5		Grey squirrel	5	
Curled dock	5		Groundsel	5	
Daisy	5		Harvestman	10	
Dandelion	5		Hedge bindweed	5	
Devil's coach-horse	10		Hedgehog	10	
Dunnock	5		Herring gull	10	
Earthworm	5		Holly	5	
Elder	5		Horse chestnut	5	
Elephant hawk moth	25		House cricket	20	
False acacia	10		Housefly	5	
Fat hen	5		House martin	10	
Feral pigeon	5		House mouse	10	
Field horsetail	20		House sparrow	5	
Fox	15		House spider	5	
Garden slug	5		Ivy	5	
Garden snail	5		Ivy-leaved toadflax	10	
Garden spider	5		Jackdaw	10	
Garden tiger moth	10		Japanese cherry	5	
German cockroach	15		Kestrel	10	
Greater plantain	5		Knotgrass	5	
Great tit	5		Laburnum	5	
Great willowherb	10		Large yellow underwing	10	
Greenfinch	10		Leaf-cutter bee	15	
Greenfly	5		Lombardy poplar	10	
Green lacewing	10		London plane	5	

Species	Score	Date spotted	Species	Score	Date spotted
Magpie	5		Silverweed	15	
Male fern	15		Six-spot burnet moth	10	
Mallard	5		Small tortoiseshell	5	
Mole	25		Small white butterfly	5	
Moorhen	10		Snake millipede	10	
Mugwort	5		Song thrush	10	
Mute swan	10		Starling	5	
Netted slug	10		Stinging nettle	5	
Painted lady	15		Sulphur tuft	10	
Parmelia physodes	10		Swallow	15	
Peacock	10		Swift	10	
Pied wagtail	10		Sycamore	5	
Pineappleweed	5		Tufted duck	10	
Pipistrelle bat	20		Two-spot ladybird	5	
Rabbit	10		Vapourer moth	10	
Red admiral	15		Wall rue	20	
Ribwort plantain	10		Wall screw moss	5	
Robin	5		Whitebeam	10	
Rosebay willowherb	5		White clover	5	
Rowan	5		White dead-nettle	5	
Scots pine	10		White wagtail	20	
Seven-spot ladybird	5		Woodlouse	5	
Shepherd's purse	5		Woodpigeon	5	
Silver birch	5		Wren	10	
Silver cord moss	5		Yarrow	5	
Silverfish	10		Zebra spider	15	

INDEX

Acacia, False, 22
Admiral, Red, 42
Ant, Black, 48
Ash, Common, 20

Bat, Pipistrelle, 36
Bee, Leaf-cutter, 44
Bindweed, Hedge, 13
Birch, Silver, 23
Blackberry, 15
Blackbird, 34
Blowfly, 45
Bluebottle,
    see Blowfly
Brachythecium Rutabulum, 53
Bullfinch, 32
Bumblebee, Buff-tailed, 44
Burnet Moth, Six-spot, 41

Centipede, 51
Chaffinch, 32
Cherry, Japanese 24
Chestnut, Horse, 23
Chickweed, 11
Cinnabar Moth, 40
Cleavers, Common, 11
Clover, White, 12
Cockroach,
    Common, 46
    German, 46
Coltsfoot, 8
Coot, 26
Coriolus Versicolor, 54
Cranefly, Common, 45
Cricket, House, 48

Daddy-long-legs,
    see Cranefly, Common
Daisy, 13
Dandelion, 8
Dead-nettle, White, 10
Devil's Coach-horse, 47
Dock,
    Broad-leaved, 17
    Curled, 17
Dove, Collared, 29
Duck, Tufted, 27
Dunnock, 33

Earthworm, 50

Earwig, Common, 48
Elder, 23

Fat Hen, 16
Fern, Male, 52
Fleabane, Canadian, 9
Fox, 39
Frog, Common, 39
Froghopper, Common, 46
Fungus, Coral Spot, 54

Goosegrass,
    see Common Cleavers
Greenfinch, 32
Greenfly, 46
Groundsel, 9
Gull,
    Black-headed, 28
    Herring, 28

Harvestman, 49
Hawk Moth, Elephant, 40
Hedgehog, 36
Holly, 25
Horsetail, Field, 52
Housefly, 45
Hoverfly, 44

Ink Cap, Common, 54
Ivy, 17

Jackdaw, 35

Kanzan,
    see Cherry, Japanese
Kestrel, 28
Knotgrass, 13

Laburnam, 24
Lacewing, Green, 45
Ladybird,
    Seven-spot, 47
    Two-spot, 47
Lichen,
    Common Orange, 56
    Grey Crust, 56
Lime, Common, 20

Magpie, 35
Mallard, 27

Mallow, Common, 14
Martin, House, 30
Millipede, Snake, 51
Mole, 36
Moorhen, 26
Moss,
    Beard, 53
    Silver Cord, 53
    Wall Screw, 53
Mouse, House, 37
Mugwort, 16

Nettle, Stinging, 16
Nightshade, Black, 11

Painted Lady, 42
Parmelia Physodes, 56
Peacock, 43
Pigeon, Feral, 29
Pineappleweed, 9
Pine, Scots, 18
Plane, London, 19
Plantain,
    Greater, 12
    Ribwort, 12
Polypore, Birch, 55
Poplar, Lombardy, 25

Rabbit, 38
Rat,
    Black, 37
    Brown, 37
Redstart, Black, 35
Robin, 31
Rowan, 21
Rue, Wall, 52

Shepherd's Purse, 10
Shrew, Common, 38
Silverfish, 48
Silverweed, 8
Slug,
    Garden, 50
    Netted, 50
Snail, Garden, 50
Sparrow, House, 33

Spider,
    Garden, 49
    House, 49
    Zebra, 49
Squirrel, Grey, 38
Starling, 31
Sulphur Tuft, 55
Swan, Mute, 27
Swallow, 30
Swift, 30
Sycamore, 19

Thistle, Creeping, 15
Thrush, Song, 31
Tiger Moth, Garden, 41
Tit,
    Blue, 34
    Great, 34
Toad, Common, 39
Toadflax, Ivy-leaved, 15
Tortoiseshell, Small, 42

Underwing, Large Yellow, 41

Vapourer Moth, 40

Wagtail,
    Pied, 26
    White, 26
Wasp, Common, 44
Whitebeam, 21
White, Small, 43
Willowherb,
    Great, 14
    Rosebay, 14
Woodlouse, 51
Woodpigeon, 29
Wren, 33

Yarrow, 10